Per-Money:
Permaculture Principles for Indie Biz Growth

Katie McCaskey

ISBN: 1507810679
ISBN-13: 978-1507810675

"Well, what are you, *high*?"

I blinked my bloodshot eyes twice. Yes. I heard the question correctly. It wasn't what I was expecting, given that I was in uncomfortable clothes and standing in the family receiving line at a funeral.

"Who starts a business in the middle of this recession mess? You must be crazy!"

I wasn't sure who the man was or what exactly he was trying to do. Change the subject? Lighten the mood? Awkward, those funeral introductions and reunions. The standby filler comment ("Great to see you!") seems wholly unwelcome in these situations. I stammered something in return while thinking, "*Who asks that, at a funeral?*"

Was he high?

I mean, *come on*, I thought, getting a bit indignant. If he was referring to a few laughs punctuated with terrorizing moments of paranoia, well, yep, sounds like business building to me.

I silently stewed watching the man make his way down the line of next-of-kin. In what social system is that question appropriate, I wondered angrily.

You see, our business was in crisis. At that moment I was questioning everything. My boyfriend and I were pretty damn sure we'd made a gigantic and costly mistake. We'd left New York City and moved to a small town in Virginia, surrounded by my family. On a bit of a whim we started a neighborhood grocery on Main Street, like the ones we'd pop into around the city.

Let's just say it wasn't going so well.

Little did I know, this man's rude comment planted a seed. I'd been obsessing about systems in general (What were we doing wrong? What were we doing right?), and his comment turned my attention to social systems. Sometimes obsessing can be good.

Thanks to this weird chance encounter my mind was ready when a new friend, Meghan asked: "Have you heard of permaculture?" I had not. Permaculture is a design philosophy that attempts to mimic Nature's wisdom. The principles are most frequently applied to sustainable agriculture (creating "permanent agriculture" or "permanent culture"). However, the principles can be applied to money and business building, too.

I started applying permaculture design thinking to running our Main Street business. It wasn't a magic bullet. But it was one of the smartest things we did to turn things upside down, and eventually, around. You can do it, too.

Per-Money:
Permaculture Principles for Indie Biz Growth

IN GRATITUDE

The permaculture design framework was developed by Australians
Bill Mollison and David Holmgren in the 1970s.

This book uses permaculture systems thinking and applies it to money
management and independent business-building. This book uses the design
principles outlined in "Essence of Permaculture" (Version 3; April 2004)
by David Holmgren as its starting point.

This book expands on these ideas through the experience of building a
Main Street, brick-and-mortar business. I wrote it because I believe
business building is a creative act that should positively influence
people, planet, and place.

WHO THIS BOOK IS FOR
(& WHOM IT WILL DISAPPOINT)

This book is for intelligent, independent thinkers who are building businesses that matter.

I define "businesses that matter" rather narrowly, and certainly differently than many mainstream interpretations. The mainstream "pro-business" discussion often revolves around businesses I abhor: those with a crushing disregard for people, planet, or place in pursuit of profit only.

I have no fondness for car-dependent, sprawl-driven businesses, either, such as the many franchises. (Although these are "independently owned" they are at the behest of decisions made at their headquarters.)

Capitalism, as typically expressed, lays waste to what truly matters.

In the "Micropolitan Manifesto" I urged entrepreneurs to locate themselves in our smallest urban areas. I am passionate about that as a means to continue the walkable revitalization, better land development strategies, and to reclaim place over homogenized commercial culture. There is still so much to do.

When I say "businesses that matter" I'm referring to micro-sized, independently owned, community-centric, local businesses.

This book does not have a political bent. If it veers, it veers neither left nor right but rather bends more toward anarchy. Yes, anarchy. *Let's go ahead and be dramatic!* We must radically reconsider how we live and use our natural resources. That fact is directly connected to how and where we live and how we spend our money.

I think place matters and culture matters. Both are being fed into a modern meat grinder that spits out mindless consumers in a never-ending pattern of consumption.

In the context of a capitalistic society, indie businesses can help redefine the direction.

So, this book is focused on "indie biz": the small and micro-sized businesses that contribute beyond the limited scope of generating tax dollars or jobs (although both are clearly important). Specifically, these are the businesses that produce one or more other, more important yields:

- Contribution to environmental stewardship and/or regeneration
- Contribution to more just, humane, or locally made options in the marketplace
- Contribution to walkable infrastructure development/re-development
- Contribution to a community's culture and unique sense of identity and place

Not enough *business-as-usual* businesses include any of these ideas on the balance sheet. More should.

Those **unfamiliar with permaculture** will, hopefully, come away with a new way of exploring how their business' systems interlock and how vital it is to have your strategy and systems work together.

Those already **familiar with permaculture** will, hopefully, enjoy thinking about these principles applied to money and business building.

For obvious reasons this book cannot give you a roadmap specific to your situation. Too many business books focus too narrowly on tactics ("Get on social media!") and forget the larger systems and overall strategy.

Instead, this book assumes you know what is best for your situation. **It is structured with one goal: to trigger ideas and give you a fresh look at your own business.**

All of the design principles are discussed. All of them overlap and interlink. Some will be more applicable to your situation at present than others. I share my own experiences of implementing these principles -- not because my business is perfect but because it provides an inside look at choices and challenges.

I am a student of permaculture and a student of business building. I expect to spend a lifetime getting better at both.

Katie McCaskey

CONTENTS

PERMACULTURE DESIGN &
THE ART OF INDIE BUSINESS

Let's clarify a few things before we get started.

The first thing to know is that applying permaculture design philosophy is not like getting LEED certification for a building. There aren't hard and fast rules about implementation. Nor does one tick off a list of items to a certain threshold in order to qualify as a "permaculture project".

Instead, permaculture is a system of thinking. It is typically applied to regenerative landscape and/or sustainable agricultural design. The process asks that we look out over a long timeline with the goal of matching needs with an outcome that positively affects everyone and everything it touches. Permaculture's highest emphasis is on stewardship of people and planet.

Applying permaculture perspective to our businesses requires deep contemplation, and sometimes very slow implementation, such as:

- How can our business fund positive people and planetary initiatives (locally and/or globally)?
- How can we incorporate practices that are more sustainable, while acknowledging our own fiscal limitations?
- How can we manage our money systematically, instead of reflexively?
- How can we provide more value outside the money system?
- How can we improve our chances of success, and extend those benefits beyond ourselves?
- How can we share the surplus?

Throughout this book I'll be sharing examples and lessons learned from George Bowers Grocery, the neighborhood sandwich shop and beer garden my husband Brian and I have started and still operate.

We are a micro-sized business located in downtown Staunton, Virginia, a tiny city three hours southwest of Washington, D.C. Our business is typically operated by two to four people during our busiest times and contracts to just one person in the winter. We took our name from a long-forgotten business that operated in the same storefront and began selling retail food.

Eventually, we moved locations and grew into a restaurant. Our business is six years old, which is long enough to surpass many failure statistics but not so old that we believe we know it all.

On the surface, your independent business might not seem to share a lot with mine. However, I do believe we share at least one common challenge. That is the challenge of a fresh perspective when we're puzzling over options.

Each of these sections will offer some "food for thought" and, occasionally, some tools. Naturally, there is no one-size-fits-all approach. You are smart enough to follow the threads that matter most to you and your situation.

DESIGN PRINCIPLE 1:
OBSERVE AND INTERACT
"Beauty is in the eye of the beholder."

Like in all great journeys, the first step is deceptively simple.

The first permaculture design principle is to "observe and interact." In a landscape context this means that prior to drawing up a design you must take into careful consideration a range of site-specific variables and conditions. What features and resources already exist? How is the land sloped? How does the sun cast its light on the site? How is water collected and stored?

The challenge is to see the site for what it is now, and predict how it is likely to behave in the future. As a designer, you must consider the resources available and make decisions that will work *with* what exists, in addition to anything new you plan to introduce. If I introduce X, what happens to Y? How does that impact Z?

The parallels to business building are clear. To succeed you need to embrace ongoing observation. You need to continuously test and tweak, building upon the decisions that are working.

Intuitively, entrepreneurs excel at seeing "what is missing" and taking massive action to put it out into their environment. Actually, we have a knack for it. The same observational energy you used to conceptualize your business is the same process you'll need to employ on a daily basis for its survival and growth. An idea plus groundwork equals a starting point. No guarantees.

Those of us with micro-sized businesses also have some keen advantages over larger corporations. For example, we have a direct connection with our customers and their feedback, whereas larger companies observe and interact through the barriers of impersonal surveys or outsourced market research firms. We can quickly implement changes without hierarchy or formality. That gives us a huge advantage to see and respond to opportunities in our neighborhoods and local communities.

Lest we think we're all that and a bag of kale chips... It is easy to veer off our road of observation and interaction.

The Game That Never Ends

Observation is a game that never ends. Yet, the first risk to your business is falling out of practice. So let's look how we can increase your capacity for observation and interaction so you can maximize your ability to spot opportunity. You should be looking at everything around you, and I mean *everything*. That includes other businesses.

Observing other businesses should become, well, second nature. Treat it like an environmental study. Your goal is a kind of bio-mimicry. How are other indie businesses choosing their assortment of goods? Presenting services? What is their service approach? How are they managing key relationships?

No, I'm not suggesting you watch like some creepy peeping Tom. Nor should you set out to duplicate anyone literally (because first of all, *ick*, and second of all, I trust you have better ideas). The point is watching with an eye to try and understand the rationale. You *can't* know all the variables but you *can* watch results. Watching others can give you insight into market conditions, needs, and feedback.

When and where appropriate you *might* -- emphasis, might -- apply a similar approach. Sometimes it makes sense to "fall in line" and other times it makes more sense to "zig while the others are zagging."

Why, for example, are all businesses downtown closed on Mondays? Is there a good reason, or is that an opportunity? The only way you can know is after you've amassed a reasonable sense of what is really going on around you. An amazing amount can be learned keeping your eyes open and your mouth shut. Don't offer others advice unless asked. As is rightly said, "Mind your own business."

What businesses should you watch? You might want to focus your attention on those with similar scale, location, or field. But, to really broaden your perspective, you'll need to actively observe businesses that have (seemingly) nothing in common with yours. That's what can really get the gears going.

An Example That Frosted My Flakes

It is worth underlining that you can look all you want but can *never really know* what's going on behind-the-scenes.

An example that frosted my flakes was a local restaurant that had the word "Irish" in the name. No, it was not an Irish food restaurant. In fact, it took great offense, and regular measures, to reiterate that it only sold "American food." Fine. Except… The main entrance was through the bar.

The world over the "Irish pub" offers a pretty consistent idea. Despite the name and the pub entrance the owners fought against this idea tooth and nail. *No! American food!*

At a certain point I wondered, why don't they just add a tap of Guinness? Hang up a flag, and start serving mashed potatoes and cabbage soup? Why not leverage our geographic area's Scot-Irish roots and give the people what they want? *No! American food!*

Were they simply out of money? Had they invested too much ego in one idea? Or, were they just unwilling to see that there were plenty of "American food" restaurants already? Why resist when people were responding, daily, to the idea of a theme? I'll never know. My point here is that I watched closely. They eventually added Guinness on tap, just before they closed.

It is said that a business plan never survives the real world, and our business was no different. We had to face up to a few misguided ideas once we really started observing our surroundings. We had overestimated foot traffic, for example. We did not appreciate that people were not in the habit of going to our location for any reason, let alone to get groceries!

Eventually we shifted our concept entirely, and that was because we put such emphasis on observation. We kept interacting with the facts as they were and building toward what we wanted in the context of what worked.

How can we consciously apply this principle of observation and interaction to your cash flow? Oh, right. *That.*

Let's talk about *that.*

Economic Gardening

If you want to watch a trippy documentary check out *DMT: The Spirit Molecule*. It looks at dimethyltryptamine (DMT), a molecule found in every organism on Earth. It is a potent psychedelic, and, yes, is partly responsible for how roots in the soil talk to one another. The film reiterates that, like roots in the soil, everyone and everything is connected.

In the economic development world that concept is expressed as "economic gardening." The idea is that each business plays a specific role in the ecosystem of a place. Every individually strong business makes the whole local economy stronger and more resilient. So, the emphasis is on "growing" independent businesses of varying sizes and capacities from within the local base. This is in contrast to the more common approach of courting outside companies with tax breaks and other expensive and often unsustainable incentives.

Cash Management Is Your Soil

If all our businesses are connected we both need to be strong. Being strong is rooted in cash flow and cash management. This is one of the hardest things to learn to control.

Permaculture design applied begins in the soil. In the business-building sense your cash flow is that soil. It may be healthy and strong. Or, it may need amendments and careful, patient care. Either way the observation and interaction with cash is a daily process.

One of the most fundamental cash flow lessons to learn is that managing cash in a business is very different from managing your personal money. Often, personal money comes from a regular source (like a job) and routed to semi-fixed expenses. By contrast, a business' cash flow varies, sometimes wildly. The number one goal of cash management for a business is to **protect your cash flow.**

A simple example: In your personal life it might make sense to buy toilet paper (or whatever else) in bulk to "save money" because you know that next Friday you'll be paid. The short-term trade of exchanging this "savings" for reduced spending is okay because you know when your reserves will be restocked.

A business's inflow of cash may be regular, or it may swing wildly. Either way, it is more important to preserve capital for known expenses given the reality of uncertain, or varying revenue. You want to avoid depleting reserves for immediate needs. This even includes those that appear to "save" money. Disrupting your cash flow for "savings" may end up costing you more in the long run.

(An environmental corollary of bad cash management is watering a golf course using water from the aquifer when you're experiencing drought.)

Applying Principle #1 to Business Finances

Some ways we **observe** and **interact** with our business finances:

Observation

- Daily cash flow in and out
- Tracking what sells, and what sells best
- Observation of seasonal trends
- Observation of similar and dissimilar businesses (Example: How others seem to be spending and investing, knowing we can't grasp the whole picture)

Interaction

- Protecting cash flow by spending strategically
- Strategizing cash outflow to best use
- Moving funds for maximum-use capacity (for example, temporarily ceasing one vendor order to address a more urgent need)
- Balancing debt service and funding growth
- Spending: making it a priority to buy goods and services in your local economy
- Sharing: intentionally giving goods and services away
- Designating funds to protect your interests

No business survives without ongoing sales. As the owner, you need to adjust your offering accordingly, which is why active observation and experimentation are foundational to success. Make it a practice to keep your eyes and ears open -- not for gossip, but for learning.

Cash management, and specifically protecting cash flow, is your number one priority. Experiment regularly. All experiments should be limited so that they don't risk toppling the business' survival.

Tools and Tactics for Observation

I love technology. I track many things on many apps and find the process valuable. For example, I use Workflowy as a way to capture ideas. However:

The number one thing you can do to increase your capacity for observation is to consciously disconnect from technology on a regular basis. The worst culprit is your smartphone. New science shows that our phones are destroying the time we need to let our minds wander aimlessly. Being "bored" is actually pretty critical to success because it allows our subconscious bubble up and offer insights. We need this time for creativity and problem solving.

Don't believe me? Download Moment (iPhones) or BreakFree (Android) to see how much time you spend on your phone. Average users check their phones 150+ times a day. Consider how much time that eats up in addition to the loss of insights you could gain.

Check out New Tech City's *Bored and Brilliant* series for more of that research.

Thought Exercises for Your Business

Observing:

- What do I see that no one else is addressing?
- How do others appear to be addressing X? What appears to be working? What isn't?
- How does my business fit into the local economic ecosystem? Environmental ecosystem?
- What isn't working as expected? In how many ways can I respond to that?
- What are the invisible structures surround my business? (e.g., social; historical; political; habitual, etc.) How can they be managed? Leveraged?
- If I (try to) remove my ego from the equation, what else do I observe? (See also: *The Subtle Art of Not Giving a F*ck*, by Mark Manson)

Interacting:

- What am I hearing when I listen? How can I listen more?

- How can I incorporate more non-cash options into my business? (e.g., sharing, borrowing, trading, bartering services?)
- How can I solve a cash issue by forgoing ownership? (e.g. renting services, tools, or other equipment versus owning them and the cost of maintaining them)
- How can my business better serve the people involved? (Customers, suppliers, connected professionals?)
- What are some ideas for symbiotic and beneficial relationships with others? Businesses, non-profits, the local environment?
- When I interact with others in the community I serve, what do I hear and see?
- What awkward or uncomfortable questions do I need to ask others? Ask myself?

Remember to disconnect regularly and let the mind wander. It is crucial for gaining insight!

DESIGN PRINCIPLE 2:
CATCH AND STORE ENERGY
"Make hay while the sun shines."

The natural world is full of examples of catching and storing energy. For example, sunlight energy is stored in chlorophyll of the plant for release as needed. Water is stored in temporary puddles until absorbed into the soil. Or consider the life potential stored in a single seed.

In permaculture design applied to landscapes we work with Mother Nature's existing patterns to maximize specific outcomes. For example, we might dig swales to accumulate and store rainwater. Or, we might position rocks to collect heat during the day for slow release at night, creating a favorable microclimate for a particular plant.

The business interpretation of "catch and store energy" is all about maximizing capital. How do we use our capital most efficiently? Most intentionally? The smaller the business the more directly you feel the up-and-down waves of cash. The key idea here is maximizing capital in a way that fits your needs and goals. It does not necessarily mean grasping for more, mistaking it for "bigger is better" (see also, Design Principle #9).

Your relationship with capital depends greatly on your perspective and unique situation. Newer businesses differ from established businesses. The thread that knits all is the practice of getting the most out of every expenditure and investment without harm to others. "Others," in an expanded view, includes the natural world.

Our business is very seasonal, in part because we have one of the few outdoor patios in town. We are busy with tourists and locals spring through fall, with a lull during the hottest dog days of summer. Winters are painfully slow, but have gotten easier with time.

Seasonal fluctuations impact everything from our hours to our menu, and, therefore, influence the cash flow. Maximizing our capital during the busy season is imperative to surviving winter. A positive outcome of this is that we choose to slow down and regroup. This is in contrast to many businesses that artificially prop up, say, with extra heating and utility costs, to capture low return.

Cash Like Clean Water

Revenue is like clean water and sunlight to a landscape. You need a regular influx of both. You also need to move it according to a proactive plan.

For most indie businesses the greatest trick is balancing two important uses of cash. The first is debt service and the second is reinvestment in business growth. Finding the correct balance is key.

Revenue should be stored for slow periods -- but, like water, shouldn't be stagnant. Some might define "stagnant" as earning very little in a savings account. It is also stagnant if placed with a large commercial bank, which has little concern for, or investment in, localities. Keeping your revenue circulating through a community bank or a credit union keeps more of it productive at the local level.

Examples of Catching and Storing Cash

Indie businesses "catch and store energy" a variety of ways to maximize capital. Here are few examples.

Catching energy, or saving expenditures, by:

- contemplating need and utility, asking, is there a way to do/accomplish this without spending money? As you practice this line of thinking more solutions will reveal themselves.

- focusing on *access*, not *accumulation*. For example, renting or sharing tools or equipment rarely used versus the expense of acquisition and maintenance. Here, social ties with other business owners are extremely beneficial.

- increasing personal skills to increase your DIY flexibility.

- looking for ways to market your business using the least amount of time and energy. For example, creating online content for someone with a broader audience than your own. More on that in a bit.

Storing energy, or saving revenue, by:

- incorporating more non-cash options into your business. This could include barter, trade, gift certificates, IOUs, jointly held ownership, group purchases, etc.

- working with patterns of cash flow (e.g. seasonal patterns) once you've observed enough to understand them. For example, not investing heavily prior to a likely slowdown in sales.

- implementing solid cash management to protect the cash flow, as discussed.

  Here's a tactic we use. We have two checking accounts for the business. One is our main account, the slush of in and out. The other is reserved for our most mission-critical monthly expenses, such as rent. We put something into the second account daily with the goal to fill it to cover those expenses as quickly as possible. Does it always remain off-limits? No, but that's the goal. Similarly, we put the bulk of our summer tips and found money (like an unexpected refund) into savings for the winter ahead.

- maximizing energy efficiencies for cost savings AND long-term growth, especially as they present weaknesses. We'll look at some ideas in Design Principle #5.

How We Get National Press

A big marketing win for our business illustrates the "catching energy" idea. It is an example of a single effort yielding ongoing results.

We don't pay for advertising but are always looking for earned media opportunities. We try to deploy efforts where there is the best potential for possible return.

I saw an opportunity to submit a business story to a popular political website (Salon.com). It cost me writing time but the returns were worth it. You see, most publications are always looking for material.

The article was published and we got a positive response. I'd be happy if it had ended there, but it didn't.

The article triggered an invitation for an interview on a nationally broadcast American Public Radio show called "The Story." It was an hour long!

Once our regional affiliate radio stations heard we'd be on the show they started running promo features to promote the episode. "Tune in for the next episode, featuring our very own George Bowers Grocery…"

Now, how much would it have cost to run an ad in *Salon*, or pay for a nationally syndicated show to talk about our business for an hour? Or even get on-air call-outs on the local airwaves? *Answer: a lot* more than our business could pay!

Similarly, we submitted a single photo and short paragraph to a call from the business section of *The New York Times, (What's black, white, and read all over?)* We were included in a big batch of other businesses, but hey, now we can legitimately say we've been in the *Times*. Both of these efforts are now reflected in our media kit.

Will all efforts yield such results? No. But more of them can, if you are consistent.

How did I find these opportunities? By consistently reserving one hour/one day/week to look for earned media opportunities -- over something I always do anyway: drinking my morning coffee. That's a habit stack.

Stacking Habits

Permaculture design frequently refers to "stacking functions," that is, making sure that every part in a system performs multiple functions, not just once, but also through time. A plant may be harvested as one part of the sequence, and its decaying foliage provides fertilizer for another.

Similarly, businesses need to smartly stack habits, or procedural outcomes, in order to create a sellable business. Perhaps selling your business is not a goal. Even so, mechanization of routine can improve your effectiveness. It does not necessarily disrupt innovation. Building systems to maximize your time and effort can be an act of creativity. It takes much experimentation to find the right balance.

Think about your existing habits and routines. How can you incorporate one business-building habit into one or more of these? Take it slow, develop a stacked habit. It will be worth your time.

Thought Exercises for Your Business

Capturing Energy

- What flows around and through my business that others don't see as a resource, but is valuable? Have I captured it? Can I reuse or share   it?

Storing Energy

- How have I built upon yesterday's successes today? (Think broadly. Successes are not always overtly monetary. For example, you may have been recognized by a peer or thanked by a customer, both of which build business trust and familiarity.)

- Have I put aside something today for tomorrow? Even just to get into the habit of doing so?

- How can I position today's efforts so they continue to grow in value?

Stacking Functions & Habits

- How can I work more effectively (versus being "busy")?

- How can I create habits that automate aspects of my business building?

- What new habit can I introduce to help me achieve a business goal? (Start small. Aim for consistency first.)

Try This

- Open a second account to retain some control of cash inflow and outflow.

- Capture and store gratitude. Sounds cheesy, but it can be a real boost. Take a moment each day to think of at least one good thing that happened in your business today. Reminders of small wins go a long way once you enter the "this is not so fun anymore" phase of business building. Try a five-minute journal app, like "Gratitude Journal," or the old-fashioned pen-and-paper. Savor surprises.

DESIGN PRINCIPLE 3:
OBTAIN A YIELD
"You can't work on an empty stomach."

As someone once said to us: "A business can't survive on good times and high fives."

Permaculture thought and design emphasize the whole system. (See: Economic Gardening in Principle #1). The whole system is successful when the individual participants within that ecosystem experience successes, too. Therefore, a good designer is always looking for ways to increase the yield, or the success, of a design to the betterment of all.

Here success is defined as dollars generated. You take cash to the bank. Not the percentages, and not the high fives. There's no arguing that we operate in a federal dollar economy. Financial yield is necessary.

Rob Hopkins, co-originator of the Transition Network wrote:

> "If Catch and Store Energy is about maximizing capital, Obtain a Yield is about income, and the observation that our businesses, our projects, need to generate a profit."

Let's look at that first.

Profit Generation and Increasing Income

Increasing income boils down to two things: More sales with better margins.

A common pitfall is pricing. Matching or undercutting a larger business' pricing is a fool's errand. No one wins in a race to the bottom, and certainly not you. Sadly, many businesses think low pricing is the answer when it is usually the problem!

For some businesses a seasonal sale to clear inventory makes sense. Otherwise, you want and need your customers to pay full price. The way to get people to pay full price is to ensure they think they are getting more in return for their money than you are. Focus on delivering dependably exceptional results.

Here are some additional offerings that can increase income and can cost you virtually nothing:

- Preview of goods or services before the general public sees it
- Personalized recommendations/custom solutions/collections
- Invitation-only workshops, training or other events (with the sales component)
- Add-ons and up-sells to existing sales

Profit Worship

Our dominant culture raises income and profit to obscene levels of worship. Big business profit is not the problem. Big business design to get and maintain the profit is the problem.

To reverse a cultural bias toward profit at all costs, we have to ask a simple but difficult question. What other business yields -- besides money -- are valuable?

Kinds of Yields

Let's take a broader view of income, or of "yield." Yields -- what a business generates -- don't always need to be monetary to be beneficial to owners, the community, and the environment. For example:

Physical yields -- These are the literal output of goods or services made possible by the business' existence.

Environmental yields -- These yields may be obvious if you are an organic farmer, but there are many ways to consider environmental yields.

17

For example, are you operating out of a renovated or reused physical space (instead of new construction)? Does your business support an environmental movement, such as sustainable food production? Or does its location help reinvigorate walkable infrastructure and reduce fuel reliance?

Knowledge yields -- These are hard won, but so valuable! As the owner, you always make decisions with the goal of avoiding mistakes, but mistakes are impossible to avoid. That's good, because mistakes are excellent teachers.

An incomplete but powerful list of what we've learned:

- how to scrutinize potential business partners (hint: DUE DILIGENCE)
- how to avoid the seduction of suppliers selling dubious wares (especially if they involve contracts!)
- how to understand broader social connections as they impact business. (For example, who has generous intentions, and who always expects special treatment or something in return?)

Knowledge yields compound. They remain beneficial moving forward as you evaluate other business opportunities.

Emotional yields -- "I've always found the term "lifestyle business" a bit derisive and dismissive of a vital category of entrepreneurs," wrote my husband in an online comment to a *New York Times* article. Yet a "lifestyle business" -- the very category favored by most indie businesses and their owners -- can give you things money can't buy: space and time for other interests, hobbies, family, or other passionate pursuits. These are yields many people seek but never find.

Social yields -- You, as an owner, probably derive a lot of satisfaction being an active contributor in your community. There are other, less obvious social yields to your efforts, too.

Conscious Consumers. Your business may help shape more conscious consumers. This can have a lasting positive impact on purchasing habits. It may contribute to positive changes to the supply chain operations, too. This can affect real, positive change.

One example of sharing yield is the idea of "suspended coffee" in Italy. Italians can choose to "pay it forward" and purchase a coffee for a stranger. Businesses allow other customers in need to redeem these coffees. What a cool thing to facilitate -- and it depends on developing conscious consumers.

Placemaking. Your indie business helps create a sense of place. "Placemaking" addresses a vital, human need to establish personal identity and tribe. Affection for, and pride in place, plays a powerful social role. Physical meeting places facilitate deeper community ties.

Economic Resilience. Lest we forget a social yield politicians love to crow about: job creation and tax revenue. Starting a business means you've created your own job. As for taxes, no one enjoys paying them, and everyone can point to an example where taxes are wasted. Yet, even those who oppose taxes benefit from their collection in some way. You can choose to reframe taxes as a positive yield, even if, admittedly, you can't directly influence how that money is spent.

Sharing Yields

When we think about yield this way we begin to understand some hopeful things. First, all indie business -- and, specifically, the people operating them -- have the choice to share. It is in fact a *choice*. Even those short on profits can choose to share something -- time, materials, introductions, friendship, or *fill-in-the-blank*.

Give freely, and on your own terms. Whatever "yield" to share is up to the business owner. I have no patience for external pressure or guilt about how I choose to share (e.g., "What do you mean you don't want to donate to my private school?").

Living Lightly Extends Income

Financial burdens reduce in proportion to how you adopt an attitude and practice of living lightly. This is a theme we'll return to frequently.

Many indie businesses struggle to reach a point where enough profit is generated to cover operational expenses in the business *and* at home. How -- and how soon -- you get to this amount of profit is specific to your set of circumstances. Assuming you aren't mainlining funds from your father's trust fund a lot of this timeline depends on your personal cost of living.

Call it simplification or minimalism or being thrifty -- just don't call it being "cheap"! Reducing lifestyle overhead is a boost to your overall bottom-line profitability. It can also significantly reduce stress and, generally speaking, is an excellent way to reduce your carbon footprint and lessen waste, too. Start by rethinking your "needs" and downsizing your consumption habits. The three largest areas to evaluate are your housing, transportation, and food.

Westerners are awash in abundance. Reducing consumption need not be a burden. In fact, as a strategy it can become enjoyable. Besides, doing so frees up cash to spend on fewer, but better quality items: organic food, American-made clothing, locally made art, etc. Readers will note these kinds of products are usually sold by independently owned businesses, supporting the regenerative circle.

A word of caution: A reduction of costs should never put you or others at risk. Think twice before a desire to reduce costs negatively impacts others. Don't be the jerk who never tips in restaurants, for example. Bad karma!

Thought Exercises for Your Business

- Where can I reduce or eliminate consumption costs at home?
- What does "yield" mean in the context of your business?
- Can part of the yield be sharing- or bartering-based (outside the money system)? If so, can you expand this area?
- Social: How can I incorporate the idea of "suspended coffee" or (something else) that shares yield, at the business level as well as the customer/client level?

DESIGN PRINCIPLE 4:
APPLY SELF-REGULATION AND ACCEPT FEEDBACK

*"The sins of the fathers are visited on
the children of the seventh generation."*

Destruction can be necessary to move forward.

The natural world is full of examples of species applying self-regulation based on feedback from the environment. For example, most species control population as food and natural resources dwindle. (We humans could do better.) The Gaia Theory posits that the entire Earth functions as organism in an ongoing feedback loop of concentric circles, from microscopic inhabitants and habitat systems on up.

The fourth permaculture design principle -- applying self-regulation and accepting feedback -- is immediately applicable to business development.

We can think about our indie businesses as a compilation of systems. There are two of particular of concern. The first is physical. We're a part of a building, a street, nested in a community, in a region, a state, and so forth. (See "Zones" in Principle #6.)

The second is personal. Just as a business exists inside concentric rings *outside* of itself the people involved in that business have to regularly and continuing look *inward* for reflection and guidance. How this is expressed to oneself and others varies; for our discussion let's focus on a secular, humanist approach and our role as environmental stewards.

First, let's talk about money again.

Self-Regulation of Your Wallet

When it comes to self-regulation of cash flow, the first step is looking at it honestly and looking at it daily. Do these two things, and you'll be miles ahead of most. The fact is, it isn't fun to look at numbers if they're going in the wrong direction. Denial won't help, though. The only way to gain some control is to know exactly where you stand.

Self-regulation of money could also include:

- Self-control: refraining from unhelpful and costly behaviors
- Self-evaluation: regular review of your finances against specific benchmarks
- Self-acceptance and forgiveness: If you've spent money foolishly and you desperately need it now, well, there is just one thing to do -- forgive yourself and move on. That money isn't coming back.

Now, let's look more closely at ourselves, since that is so closely tied to how we relate to our business finances.

The "business of self" is a topic too big and too important to explore here. Yet, we can always ground the "who we are" with "what our business contributes" by asking ourselves: Are we operating this business, and every part of it, with the best alignment of our values? What exactly *are* our values? Where and why do we draw lines?

Of course, no one, and no business, is perfect. The more important thing to consider is, am I moving in a trajectory toward an ideal? Do I continue to make incremental improvements toward that ideal?

Self-Regulation of You

A well-designed system self regulates. So does a well-adjusted, mature person.

Self-regulation starts with an accurate evaluation of self. Your sense of self can be easily distorted. It can be distorted in a negative way, through extreme stress. Or it can distort in the opposite direction if you take your accomplishments too readily and without appreciation for the advantages you have over others. (Yes, I firmly believe you have advantages -- experiences, innate talents, and so forth -- I don't, and vice-versa).

To counter these risks of distortion you must know yourself well. To be frank, a lot of us have only a surface understanding of ourselves. Sometimes the pressures of a business can really provide beneficial learning in this regard.

You should intentionally surround yourself with people who are grounded enough not to indulge your view too much one way or another.

If you are in business with your partner, as I am, both partners need to possess self-awareness and maturity. It helps to have close friendships outside the business world as a counter balance. To see and know yourself you need many mirrors.

A permaculturalist view of self-regulation includes setting limits on our business' consumption of natural resources, materials, and overall "stuff." As mentioned in Principle #3, when business (and personal) needs are simple they require less time, effort, and cost to maintain.

If there is one message in this book it is to look at your life, and your business, with an eye toward maximizing mutually beneficial, interrelated systems. Often this includes simplification. Simplification is just one tool, but it can be one of the most powerful competitive advantages for its ability to focus our attention. Another advantage is that a "simple living" approach tends to provide environmental stewardship benefits, too. One fewer car means significant expenses savings and bottom-line benefits, for example.

Our experiences with self-regulation and feedback weren't easy. It is difficult to get harsh feedback. One mentor said, "Now is not the time for self-righteous indignation!" There can be twists and turns that take all forms of control to keep our cool.

This has parallels to the natural process of succession. In nature the first plants prepare the soil and microclimate. This sets the stage for later arrival of new species of flora and fauna. Yet, flora and fauna do not arrive without destruction of the first process. Forest fires are necessary for some seeds to sprout, for example.

Similarly, our first location toughened us in a way that was necessary for our business to survive. We discarded people and processes and remade ourselves from retailer to restaurant. We needed almost total destruction to come back stronger than ever. Our second location, combined with our earlier experiences, made this possible.

Discovering and Embracing Boundaries

Self-reflection and self-regulation will shine a light on boundaries. This is good. It is natural and helpful to have limits.

Boundaries and limits can be self-determined. For example, setting financial donation goals for your business, or limiting how much you incorporate less than perfect solutions into your business.

Or, they can be external pressures, such as lack of funds. Lacking funds can spark creative thinking and solutions. Art, and indie businesses, shine with constraints. Constraints keep us focused on maximizing utility and solving problems creatively.

Boundaries require proactive problem solving. For example, our leanest winter months at the start of the year are also our most costly. One non-negotiable expense is renewal of our alcohol and beverage control (ABC) license. We must prepare for this cost during our busy season and set these funds aside untouched. Or, it means we need to hustle a solution, quick!

Feedback, But From Whom?

Who should you take feedback from? The short answer is everyone. The more accurate answer is "everyone, but with a grain of salt." It is vital to be open to outside perspectives. Yet, we must learn to accurately gauge what (if anything) may be influencing the feedback. Harder still is casting our egos aside.

Entrepreneurs naturally assume they know what is needed. We can look at this as both a strength and weakness in our own design. To counteract it we must set up processes that allow inflow of new ideas and novel perspectives. That keeps us mentally active and competitive. Yet, we must consider outflow, too. Discarding feedback is just as important a skill to learn.

Probably the hardest feedback to swallow (and excrete, if we're following nature's protocol) is the kind of feedback that kicks you in the teeth: the feedback that questions if you know what you're doing. This is the kind of feedback, public or private, that says, "If you were really doing X, you should be doing Y."

The best way to deal with that is a strong sense of self. Negative feedback will still hurt. However, consider the source of the feedback. Frankly, there will always be more critics than doers. There are always a million reasons why not. Take solace in that and remember your reason why. What you internalize as accurate or relevant is ultimately up to you. See Principle #11 for two helpful phrases to use when you get feedback.

How to Improve Your Self-Regulation

How you manage yourself and keep your sanity is wholly personal. Here are some helpful tips that apply to nearly everyone:

- Lengthy walks and talks help you process and prioritize
- Exercise reduces stress and encourages clear thinking

Less obvious are the harder questions to ask yourself on an ongoing basis:

- What role did I play in problem X? (Humility)
- Am I willing to admit I need to go in a new direction? How can I pivot? (Flexibility)
- How can I simplify process X? (Simplicity)*

* Brian simplified his daily uniform to jeans from Goodwill and promotional beer t-shirts!

Specifically, you might ask yourself:

- Is there any area in my business that is excessive, or over capacity?
- Have I placed too much emphasis on one area, to the detriment of others?
- What needs to change?
- Am I brave enough to make those changes?

How to Deal With Feedback

Feedback comes to us in many forms -- some unsolicited, some purchased, and some sought. The most important factor is to find the people in your life who will give you honest and compassionate feedback. You don't want bootlickers. Listen to all but critique all, too.

If feedback is particularly nasty (common online) do not engage with the person. People need attention for all sorts of unfixable reasons. Ignore them. Life is too short.

Some required processing of feedback:

- Am I willing to hear bad news (and respond in a measured way)?
- Have I selected the right mentors? The best peers?
- How do I know that I am progressing at a manageable pace? What will prevent me from making changes prematurely, or giving up too soon?
- Have I listened to people whose opinions differ from my own?
- Have I turned over these ideas in my head with an open mind?

DESIGN PRINCIPLE 5:
USE & VALUE
RENEWABLE RESOURCES & SERVICES
"Let nature take its course."

The fifth principal of permaculture design is to value and use renewable resources.

We know renewable resources, like wood, have quicker regenerative loops than their non-renewable counterparts, like plastic. Wood is renewable whereas plastic exists forever, even after resource-intensive recycling (no matter what the industry claims). Materials matter.

Again, nature provides the template permaculture design attempts to replicate. With respect to renewables, consider these natural functions: leaf litter turning into soil, mushrooms springing forth from decomposition, or clover growing up from the soil and simultaneously pushing necessary nitrogen into it. All are cyclical.

As business owners we should be working *with* nature's processes and abundance instead of thinking we can *replace* these processes.

Businesses -- by themselves, and by influencing their supply chains -- have ongoing opportunities to shift behavior and ultimately create more environmentally favorable outcomes. Our money should be spent thinking about how we can strengthen environmental initiatives. (This can be tricky; do your research.)

Let's look at this principle from two perspectives. The first is the "easy wins," the everyday behaviors we can do for environmental stewardship. These actions feed smart business growth thanks to reduced costs. The second is more abstract but no less important, which is to look at social ties as they relate to business. Ideally, your social connections can be managed as a renewable resource -- if you give first, and without the expectation of return!

Easy Wins

At the risk of sounding like every "Top 10 List of Things to Make Your Business More Sustainable" here's a peek at some of the ways our business strives to incorporate this design principle.

We rent our business location, therefore we have some constraints. Even so, we've implemented the following commonplace strategies in support of valuing and using renewable resources. Similar tactics may be suitable for you. Hopefully you can do even more!

- Using local recycling services -- it is amazing how many businesses do not
- Installing dimmable LED lights
- Installing low water-flow taps, and watering our indoor plants with water people don't drink
- Installing energy film on our windows, and draft dodgers in the winter. The film blocks solar gain in the summer and insulates in the winter, lessening energy use.
- Minimizing our driving, both in our commute and our supply chain
- Shutting off and unplugging lights at night
- Reusing plastic bags, beer boxes, and other packing material
- Outfitting our business equipment and decor with "used" items versus new items. We view this as both cost savings and environmental savings.

Some restaurant-specific approaches we take include composting and switching from plates to reusable woven baskets. We serve our food in baskets lined with paper that doubles as "to go" wrapping. This reduces "to go" materials and saves washing.

Where we save energy and resources we save money. It is surprising more businesses do not place sustainability higher on their list of priorities, even though some methods require upfront investment.

Are we perfect? No. Here's an example. We offer tap water as a drink, for free. Yet, there is tremendous demand for bottled water and people refuse tap water. We don't like the commodification of water. However, making a profit allows us to continue supporting the infrastructure of local, sustainably produced food. So, we compromised and decided to sell bottled water but we drew the line at plastic bottles. All of our bottled water is in glass that gets recycled.

Similarly, not all of the food we sell is locally produced. What matters is that we are able to include local food options and make a priority of adding more as we are able and as the market supports it.

Likely your business won't be perfect, either, but doing what you can is important.

One Important Question

The number one question to ask yourself is, "Are my business' required inputs being sustainably managed?" Only you know your supply chain and its weaknesses. Look for points of weakness, such as: reliance on fuel, dependence on a particular supplier, or on certain market conditions you cannot control. What can you do to lessen these threats? How can you value renewable options along the way?

Fiscally speaking, we emphasize renewables when we repay our loan back to our community bank and local microlender. This behavior recycles our money to other local businesses, increasing the economic resilience of our community. It also happens when we pool our financial resources with others. For example, when we make group purchases with other businesses or participate in common promotional events. It is difficult to overstate the importance of building and maintaining social ties.

As Hubspot founder Dharmesh Shah tweeted:

"Your probability of success is proportional to the number of people that want you to succeed. Work to keep increasing that number."

Social Ties As a Renewable Resource

Writes Holgren:

"We can also broaden the concept of renewable resources to include things like goodwill and trust, things which a business can rebuild with good husbandry. Most business doesn't just depend on law and competition, **trust is at the heart of much business and it is very much a renewable resource**." (Emphasis added.)

As is frequently cited, it takes years to build trust and moments to break it. All business owners know it is more valuable to sell to regular customers than be in a position of always acquiring new customers. Taking the view that *customers* are a renewable resource underscores the importance of service and exceeding expectations.

This isn't to say the customer is always right. Sometimes they can behave like entitled jerks. Rather, always keep your focus on your core customers and do whatever is necessary to keep *them* happy.

This was illustrated in our business one summer when we "banned" an out-of-town visitor who all but flipped over tables because she was so impatient waiting for a Reuben sandwich. (Why people lose their minds over trivial things is beyond my understanding.) She returned the following summer to discover that, yes, she was still banned because of her behavior the year before. Needless to say, she was incredulous.

Our position is simple: If you are going to disturb our regular patrons you are not welcome here. In the end she pleaded her case and we lifted the ban -- she ate with us daily for the duration of her annual stay. The point here is that we were willing to forgo her business if she caused trouble because we prioritize the comfort of our core supporters.

Everyone deals with a nasty client or customer at some point. Here, too, you must let nature take its course. You've got to trust that people are smart enough to draw their own conclusions.

Thought Exercises for Your Business

- What resources, social or environmental, do you consume on a regular basis? How can you feed back into the system? Protect the resource?
- Where are the weakest areas of your business? Can you eliminate them? Strengthen them?
- What areas of your business still rely on fossil fuels? On water quality? On other natural resources? What changes can you make to lessen this reliance?
- How can you make your business more resilient against outside forces?

- How are you investing in your relationships to strengthen your social ties?
- How are you showing customers that you value them?
- How are you letting nature take its course?

Tools

The "Internet of Things" is just rising on the horizon. These "smart" items can be linked together to control energy costs. For example, I use programmable outlet switches to control lights and turn on burglary deterrents. Check out the site "If This, Then That" (ifttt.com) for free recipes, or contribute your own.

No gadgets? No problem. Many more meaningful environmental gains can be had by carefully evaluating your business's processes and your personal behavior.

DESIGN PRINCIPLE 6:
PRODUCE NO WASTE
"A stitch in time saves nine."

"Nature doesn't have a design problem. People do."

William McDonough and Michael Braungart nailed it with this quote in the book, "Cradle to Cradle," which advocates design as a solution to environmental damage. Permaculture philosophy considers all waste as input into a self-managing system. If "waste" exists it is due to bad system design.

If we want our businesses to become self-managing systems -- that is, sellable assets -- we need to adjust our view of waste. To do so, we have to drop the idea that waste is only the byproduct of a linear system that produces one thing. If waste is an "output" we also have to reconsider our "inputs."

So Many Forms of Waste

The kinds of waste a small, indie business produces vary considerably. Even so, we can group them into common categories:

Physical waste -- it's straightforward enough. We should start by asking ourselves, how can we minimize or repurpose these leftovers?

Financial waste -- it is impossible not to waste money, especially in the beginning of a business where the learning curve is highest. Rather than think of this money as simply "gone" can we take the time to consider lessons learned?

Time waste -- participating in unnecessary meetings, badly run volunteer efforts, or other distractions. No one knows how you waste your time more than you.

Mental/Emotional waste -- simplified as obsessing about one detail, person, or event as way to feel in control. See also: hanging onto resentments, and participating in petty scorekeeping.

Waste - in Space and Time

Waste creeps in, and becomes more urgent to address, beyond the day-to-day if you consider the space and time effect. In short: it amplifies. A few minutes wasted turns into hours, a few boxes grow into a storehouse of "stuff."

For example, in our business we have a much larger volume of compostable "waste" during our busy season. We treat this "waste" as a resource and use it to amend our garden soil at home. We cart the compostable items home in a series of plastic 2-lb coffee containers with lids (themselves pulled from a recyclable bin set to the curb). We could, in theory, grow tomatoes in this amended soil and cycle these through our restaurant, too. That wouldn't work for the volume we use, but it is illustrative of the cyclical view required.

What "waste" in your business can be redirected to another use?

Modularity and Flexibility

Reducing waste, and its associated disposal costs, come down looking at your business systems to increase their modularity and flexibility. When we were a hybrid retail grocery/food service business all of our retail did "double duty" appearing on both shelf and plate. This was great for meeting minimum order requirements and using perishables quickly. (Ultimately, though, we discontinued our retail because it made our food service too expensive for what the market would bear.)

Another example is the reuse of beer boxes. We always keep boxes on hand for people who buy more than two six packs and other generalized heaving and hoeing of stuff. We also use them to deliver snacks and brown-bag catering, two "outside sales" services we do to diversify our income.

Outside sales offset our slow sales months. In that context, reusing the "waste" of boxes becomes a necessary "input" to deliver these additional sales.

Thought Exercises for Your Business

Physical waste
- Can any waste in my production or service process be eliminated? Reused or repurposed?
- Can I create something useful from it?
- Can I make money from the waste?

Financial   *waste*
What lessons have I learned from money "wasted"? It could be feedback from the marketplace. Or, it could be a lesson in dealing with vendors or other people.
- How can I protect my interests next time?
- How can I use my money with greater intentionality next time?
- How can I make it stretch further next time?

Time waste
You already know the time wasting people and circumstances in your life and business. Thinking about how to minimize these effects is half the battle. If you want a view of how you waste time on your computer and other devices, check out RescueTime.com. Or, as mentioned in Principle #1, install an app to see how much time you spend on your smartphone or tablet. Couldn't that time be used more effectively?

Mental/Emotional waste
- How can I "stack functions" to work most effectively?
- How can I burn off stress constructively? (e.g., exercise)
- How can I release unhelpful anger? (What you hold can hold you back.)

DESIGN PRINCIPLE 7:
DESIGN FROM PATTERNS TO DETAILS
"Can't see the forest for the trees."

How easy it is to get stuck in the tactics instead of the strategy!

The seventh permaculture design principal is internalizing the big picture and using that understanding to plan and execute the details. Bees are an example in nature. Each bee has its own role and acts with independent, self-determination (tactics). Yet, the hive performs in mass cooperation, almost as a single organism, to survive (strategy). Both are necessary.

This design principle circles back to observation and interaction (design principle one) with an eye toward holistic and divergent thinkers. David Holmgren writes that this design principle, applied to business, must allow:

> "[S]pace for Devil's advocates, for black sheep, for hearing the voices of those outside the dominant culture of the organization and secondly by looking from a holistic perspective of how things interconnect, rather than just relying on experts who are embedded in detail."

Businesses must grasp surrounding patterns and offer solutions that meet market demand. There *must* be a balance between the big-picture thinking and respect for the details. Too much of one or the other is a disaster.

The good news is that lots of "big picture" people are naturally drawn to entrepreneurship. Many rely on intuition. Both of these qualities make it easier to see and understand patterns. Later we can fill in the details either by hiring specialized expertise or through informal learning with mentors and peers.

Zoning In

One useful permaculture framework transferrable to business building is the concept of zones. Think of these as concentric circles emanating from the home. Rather than think of these zones as physical locations with unique considerations (as per permaculture), it is helpful to use this framework to think in terms of business tasks, mission, and place.

Broadly, these zones are:

Zone 0 -- Your business' physical location. The emphasis here is to reduce energy, conserve resources, harvest yield, etc... Topics we've discussed. You may be the only one to see operational choices and decisions made here.

In Zone 0 you want to evaluate your physical environment and ask: How can I maximize space for greatest efficiency and protection of resources? Resources, defined here, are both natural resources, and/or fiscal resources. You may need assistance or feedback regarding the best use of fiscal resources. You want to increase the frequency that you are able to deploy your fiscal resources for greatest impact. Sometimes emotions get in the way!

In our space, for example, we have a very small kitchen. It is about twelve feet long and six feet wide. That entire footprint holds our three-bay sink, deli slicer, refrigerators, assembly prep surface, and cook surfaces.

We looked at the existing "landscape" of power outlets and reconfigured the layout to streamline prep space, water usage, and increase production speed. To do this, we had to discard elements others had insisted we "needed." Adjustments were the result of paying attention to our workflow and figuring out where we could shave seconds and/or accomplish more in limited space. This rearranging informed our menu, and ultimately our profitability, too.

Another example from our business is the decision to leave our dining floorplan as modular as possible. This allows us to rearrange swiftly to accommodate diners or host special events. Being able to do both offers greater resiliency to our cash flow (with greater sandwich sales during the day, and "After Hours Bowers" events at night).

Zone 1 -- These are the daily, or more frequent, tasks and duties required to operate. These tasks may be repetitive. Or, they may require similar approach but yield different results. These are core tasks necessary to produce the product or service you provide. Most of these are hidden from the customer view.

Zone 2 -- These are the regular, perhaps weekly, tasks required to operate. For example, paying payroll or gathering fresh supplies. These too are largely outside of customer view.

Zone 3 -- These are the systems you develop. These systems group the tasks of Zones 1 and 2 in pursuit of a strategy. For example, you might have a seasonal sales strategy. Your daily and weekly goals (culmination of zones 1 and 2) work to support this strategy. Here, outsiders can begin to take stock of what's going on, for better or worse. Every business has a public component, especially community-facing ones.

Zone 4 -- This is your business as seen exclusively from the outside. Marketing people love this zone because how you are seen by others is (somewhat) malleable.

Zone 5 -- This your business in context to neighbors and peers, as determined by actual customers, clients, and patrons. Zone 5 is where your business' value is determined. It is the role, and value, others assign to your business. This is where the sales are (or are not) made.

An aspect of Zone 5 underappreciated by entrepreneurs is the role of community habit. If you are working *with* an existing pattern of habit, say, when people habitually go downtown on weekends, you're working "with the flow" and will have an easier time of it because you're not asking people to change their behavior. Conversely, if you have set up shop in an area that has been largely unused, or goes against the grain of community habit, you're pushing *a lot* harder.

Outside a Habit Zone?

We learned the effect of habits the hard way at our first location. Although technically on Main Street, our location was more "neighborhood" than "downtown." We had significantly less foot traffic because locals were not in the habit of walking there for food. Moreover, it was too far off the familiar path for tourists. Had we looked more closely at this habitual pattern we'd have selected a more expensive but better positioned storefront from the start.

If you find yourself outside a habitual zone, don't despair. This doesn't have to be a business killer. In fact, a "bad" location shows a vision of what isn't there but what is possible (and what greater hallmark to creative entrepreneurship than that?!).

That said, once you recognize this limitation you need to redouble your efforts in *all categories*. It is unrealistic to think you can change other peoples' habits simply by showing up. Frankly, no one will care. You can, however, slowly change habits if what you do or sell is remarkable enough to attract early adopters and trendsetters. These folks love a find, and love sharing their finds. What is tricky, then, is maintaining your appeal to the handful of these important people while simultaneously outliving the inevitable wait until everyone else catches up.

The good news: The earlier you recognize the patterns around you the sooner you can compile a strategy to overcome it and implement the details that make it possible. For example, we shifted from food retailer to hybrid retailer/cafe and finally to cafe/restaurant.

Zone Takeaways

Some permaculture practitioners include two more zones at each extreme: Zone 00, prior to Zone 0, and Zone 6, outside of Zone 5. Zone 00 represents the hearts of the people involved and Zone 6 explores the relationship and impact of a single house (or in this case, business) on the larger world.

What's interesting to think about here is that we as owners only really have control over the first three zones. After that, the market decides. The first two zones are filled with tactics, but we can chase our tails if we haven't stepped back to see the patterns around us and formulate a strategy. Often, this strategy differs from what we thought was appropriate at the onset. Seek to see the pattern first, then the details.

To maximize success we need to look closely at the first three zones. The most important is Zone 00. Patterns and details matter here, too.

Zone 00

In the Principle #4 chapter we talked about self-regulation as an important cornerstone to business building. It is helpful to expand that to include an understanding of our personal preferences and patterns, and work *with* these tendencies instead of against them.

For example, what's your most productive time of day? You want to deploy maximum effort toward the most important daily task(s) when you are sharp. Leave the repetitive or less taxing tasks prior to your morning coffee or postponed till the end of the day.

Here, too, patterns help. For example, in "The Essential 14 Day Guide to Cutting Your Working Hours & Increasing Your Impact" British entrepreneur Mark Asquith recommends dividing your day's tasks into the three "I's" (Important, Interesting, Integral). Focus first on accomplishing the important. Important tasks that lead to tangible, positive results. (Or, as discussed here, "Zone 1" and "Zone 2" activities.)

Chunking helps, too. Chunking, you ask? What processes can be sequenced together (stacked) for maximum effect? For example, perhaps you can combine all errands on one day or trip. This saves time and also respects planetary resources. Find the chunks that work. Replicate.

Ultimately, we want to develop personal systems that yield the best results with the least amount of effort. It saves our sanity, and frees us to focus on the business at hand. This is explored further in Design Principle #9.

Think about your own patterns of transportation, movement, eating, working, and sleeping. All of these internal rhythms can be intentionally directed to benefit your business.

Thought Exercises for Your Business

Zones
- How can I design/rearrange the physical space of my business so it is the most efficient?
- How can I arrange it so it uses the least amount of natural resources? Fiscal resources?
- Have I reconsidered my strategy in light of recognizing patterns?

Patterns

Stepping back to see patterns:

- What is the #1 social/environmental/etc. problem I'm working to fix through the medium of my business?
- How does my business fit into, and support, larger systems (watershed, local food, local economy, etc.)?
- Why does it matter?
- Why is this important to me, personally?
- Has anything changed?
- What habitual patterns exist in the community?
- How can I work with these instead of against them?

Stepping forward to develop patterns:

- How can I apply pattern thinking to my business? For example, from market evaluation to store display?
- What seed(s) can I plant today?
- What can I do today for a better tomorrow? Next week? Next year?
- What can I do today with this business to benefit people I'll never meet? (Could be conservation, could be something else.)

DESIGN PRINCIPLE 8:
INTEGRATE RATHER THAN SEGREGATE
"Many hands make light work."

The permaculture design principle "integrate rather than segregate" is of paramount importance to business because it involves one theme: resilience.

All healthy ecological systems function with resilience -- survival -- as a primary goal.

Here, the connections *between* elements are as important as the elements connected because the sums of the whole creates a more robust system. As discussed in Principle 7: Design From Patterns to Details, all of our businesses operate amongst existing social, political, and other systems. We must accept all parts of our surroundings for what they are, regardless of what we may wish them to become, because this acceptance of what *is* gives us a firm foundation to build *what's possible*.

To build a resilient business every element must contribute in more than one way.

Which Came First, the Chicken or the Checkbook?

It is helpful to use a permaculture design solution to illustrate. Let's look at chickens. Yes, chickens.

Industrial-scale chicken production includes some of the worst animal abuses here in the U.S., to say nothing of the potential for disease and degraded quality of the meat and eggs. (But hey, it's "cheap," right?)

Compare that to small-scale families and farms that use an "integrated chicken" (permaculture) approach. Here, scale is intentionally limited so as not to sacrifice the animal well-being, health, or product quality.

The U.K.'s Permaculture Association explains:

> "Many conventional and industrial systems tend to look at 'elements' (e.g. a chicken) as producing only one yield (eggs or meat). This single yield is then promoted and extended often at a cost to the environment and the element itself. In a permaculture system we are trying to utlise all the different functions and yields of an element, e.g. a chicken can provide pest control, tillage, meat, feathers, eggs, heat etc., to increase the overall yields and create a more integrated system."

Chickens can contribute in multiple ways in a manner that supports their innate "chickenness" says my local farmer and supplier, Joel Salatin of Polyface Farms. Salatin uses a moveable "egg-mobile" that moves the chickens daily so they may benefit from fresh pasture.

Chicken "waste" enhances the soil with fertilizer. Healthier soil, in turn, grows more nutritious plants for the benefit of livestock and people. It is an enclosed, circulating system that uses thoughtful design.

We need to think of our businesses and the money that flows through them with a similar multi-use, multi-benefit emphasis.

Applying Integration to Money

Some examples of ways an indie business could incorporate the idea of "integration" into their money management could include:

- Conserving/reducing costs in one area in order to spend "more" to integrate a local product or service

- Choosing to support local credit unions, community-based banks, and microlenders for funding so that debt repayment is circulated back into the local economy

- Choosing to invest beyond our business, either in investments we hold and control, or, by contributing to local-level needs

- Collaborating with other businesses to acquire goods or services or other mutually beneficial resource.

Applying Integration to Indie Business Building

Similarly, an indie business might approach "integration versus segregation" in the following business-building ways:

- Optimizing the element(s) that are working before extending resources into other areas

- Looking at every need in terms of function -- Why do I need it? What does it do? -- and thinking of other ways to accomplish the task at hand

- Consciously tending to our social web with a give-first-and-without-expectation-of-return attitude.

Maximizing Beneficial Relationships

Note the overlap: Business building and permaculture design both rely on the art/science of maximizing beneficial relationships in a reciprocal fashion.

As discussed in Principle #5: Value Renewable Resources, we can think of our customers as a kind of renewable resource if we care for their needs on a regular basis. The same can be said for every other relationship connected to our business: employees, investors, suppliers, even other supporters such as family and close friends.

How, then, can we be stewards to these relationships in a healthy way? How can we build social resilience knowing it has a positive net effect on our business' resilience, too?

You've observed that these questions are not the cultural norm in most business-building discussions.

Holmgren discusses the design principle of "integrate versus segregate," such as:

- Each element performs many functions

- Each important function is supported by many elements

If we switch "element" for the word "person" and "function" for "business"* (*community-based, independent business, as we define here):

- Each person performs many businesses (Point 1)
- Each important business is supported by many people (Point 2)

Point 1: "Performs many businesses." You've heard the overused phrase that business owners must "wear many hats," and you know it is true. Owners must first work hard to be remarkable in their primary function (whatever they actually do/sell). They must also hustle and learn how to be effective and functional at several other unrelated but important tasks.

Ask yourself, where am I struggling? Who can I rely on who may have the answers, given their unique experience, perspective, specialization, or expertise?

Ask them for help. Seriously. Ask them.

The best way to build social resilience is to be generous and trustworthy -- first! If you sincerely demonstrate both qualities you will *always* have people come to your aid when it is needed. Ask for help because everyone likes giving the gift of being useful and valuable.

The reader will be sorely disappointed to discover this is not the case if you've asked for too much, too frequently, or without a measure of gratitude.

Social resilience starts with you and what you give.

Point 2: Visible and invisible networks of people are necessary for any business to succeed. Culturally we celebrate the competition and, to some degree, the win-at-all-costs, predatory model of business. We must infuse business with a more collaborative, mutualistic success model.

Competition, Redefined

Never fear another business. This is especially true if the business appears to be similar to yours. To worry, gripe, and moan leads to foolish and petty decisions. You'll be blinded to greater potential.

We've had several experiences that demonstrate "integrate" instead of "segregate" and we try to pay this attitude forward. We've combined orders with other businesses to make minimums. When we determined fresh produce wasn't viable for us, we teamed with a farmer and became his CSA (Community Supported Agriculture) box drop location. We've had other restaurants -- our "competition" -- loan us equipment in a pinch. If you think creatively, you can work with the "competition" and both end up stronger.

If there is a "Them" to oppose it is not another independent business owner. "We" are all in this together.

Thought Exercises for Your Business

Financial
- How else can I invest at the local level?
- How can I pool resources with others so we both reduce costs?
- How can I move my money to more productive use?

Social
- How can I give first?
- How can I give without expectation of reciprocation?
- How can I selflessly serve another business owner I know?

Business building
- How can I integrate additional revenue channels that are aligned with my core values and current offerings?
- What are my points of weakness? Areas where I dependent? Can I find ways to incorporate others that results in a more resilient situation?
- What are the examples of lateral integration in my business? In other words, how can I strengthen those (social/environmental/other) ties that aren't directly connected to what I sell?

DESIGN PRINCIPLE 9:
USE SMALL AND SLOW SOLUTIONS
"Slow and steady wins the race."

Contrary to dominant business-building thinking, there are reasons to limit growth.

Capitalism without constraint is cancerous to people and planet because, when driven to extremes, it values neither. As capitalism destroys the Commons we all lose. How can we think and behave differently?

The ninth permaculture design principle is that of "small and slow." The idea is perfectly illustrated with fertilizer. Fertilizer provides plants with better nutrition and growth over a sustained period. However, dumping excessive fertilizer into the soil can kill.

Excessive growth is bad for plants because juicy new flesh makes them more vulnerable to pests. Fast, excessive growth of businesses can be just as fatal. Growth can be an abstraction and hard to evaluate in big business -- what's a billion here, a billion there? Yet it is plainly evident in micro-sized, indie businesses. Too many get caught in the trap of "bigger is better" for vanity's sake and then can't sustain their business.

As a business owner you've got to ask yourself three things. How big do I want my business to be? How fast do I want to grow? Do I want it to keep growing?

The Hardest Thing in Business to Get Right

Scale is the most critical part to get right. Bigger isn't always better -- but small isn't the right choice by default, either. You can "business plan" and "market research" all you want, but at the end of the day your choice of scale meets the realities of the market. All you can do is hope to adjust quickly enough.

Some examples:

Physical Scale

Is your business the right physical size for the volume of customers you serve? Too small, and you might not survive, let alone grow. Too big, and you risk a lack of demand to support the overhead. If possible, think of ways your physical space can flex to accommodate your needs. Walls might initially make a space scale appropriate to meet your needs. These could be removed later to provide space to grow into without undue expense, for example.

Our business' physical size expands seasonally, effectively doubling seating capacity in the warm months.

Fiscal Scale

How does money flow into your business, and how is it used? Are you spending that money in a way that strengthens your business and community? Or are you borrowing here to pay there, operating on a credit-enhanced scale that is unsustainable?

One vital part of scale is a manageable debt load. Sure, operating without debt is ideal but not always practical. Assuming you have debt it may be more realistic and less risky to pay slowly, in small amounts, than empty the coffers in one go and be left in a vulnerable cash flow position.

Every time we've been tempted to do a push-up and pay off something quickly has been a mistake because it disrupted cash flow. The balance between growth and debt service must be deliberate. It requires a lot of patience because seeing marked differences in either direction can be slow moving. Yet, a slow approach means we remain stable and continue to get stronger and more profitable over time. Again, living lightly, as mentioned in Principle #3, goes a long way.

Time Scale

Are you expecting a quick flip? Or do you have a slow and steady vision with a long time commitment? Most indie businesses need to consider the latter to build lasting equity.

Do you want your business to survive you? You must think deeper than mainstream business conversation dictates.

Scale as Opportunity

Mollison and Holmgren state that "systems should be designed to perform functions at the smallest scale that is practical and energy-efficient for that function."

Small scale can be an opportunity to serve very niche audiences bigger business won't touch. If you're trying to do this on Main Street you may need an online sales component, too. Either way, it is helpful to look at your size as an advantage, not a disadvantage.

Many indie businesses find the best and widest opportunities at smaller scales with devoted local markets and comparatively lower overhead. Recent years have seen an explosion in craft brewing and artisanal foods, as an example.

Thought Exercises for Your Business

- Am I building beyond what business or community can actually support?
- How can I scale up or down?
- How can I resisting debt financing, if possible? If debt is necessary, can I choose options that do the most good, such as using a community-owned bank or credit union?
- How am I keeping my focus and commitment over a long time horizon?
- How can I slowly and deliberately make adjustments toward a goal, without disruption?

DESIGN PRINCIPLE 10:
USE & VALUE DIVERSITY
"Don't put all your eggs in one basket."

The song "America the Beautiful" has the well-loved lyrics, "from sea to shining sea." If written today the lyrics might be "from sea to shining Applebee's." American culture has increasingly become a drab mix of sameness, a "Generica" comprised of the same chain restaurants and strip malls from coast to coast. Worse, we're infecting other countries.

If there is *one* reason to have an indie biz it is to fight this onslaught of cultural monoculture.

Monocultures are fragile and prone to disease and pests. They do not occur in nature. Man-made monocultures -- including our consumer consumption culture -- require considerable input of human work, fuel, and (oil-derived) chemicals. Also: The results are *so* boring.

Centralized business systems are globalization's version of monoculture.

Permaculture design Principle #10 -- use and value diversity -- is a business no-brainer because with luck and diversification you can better insure yourself against random misfortune. This builds on Principle #8 (Integrate vs. Segregate) for increased resilience.

Our businesses need diversity expressed two ways: variety and possibility balanced with productivity and power.

Variety and Possibility in Business Building

Variety is what separates a run-of-the-mill business from another. Not in terms of product assortment but in terms of experience. One of the best advantages indie businesses have is the ability to offer a unique experience (variety!) not found in every other place. That's the system strategy viewed from the outside, viewable by customers and the public. Offering an alternative to the norm is where we win.

There are numerous ways to express variety.

One way is to think about variety through your sales strategy and resulting combinations. For example, our business offers a narrow band of products (sandwiches, burgers, beer, non-alcoholic beverages). Although small, we have the following variety of sales configurations, each serving a specific audience or circumstance:

- craft beer enthusiasts vs. non-drinkers
- burgers vs. vegetarian
- snack vs. meal
- on-site vs. off-site (e.g., catering, outside snack sales)

These combos offer a diversity of price points and experiences, too. Some businesses may benefit from other sales diversification combos, such as:

- one-off vs. subscription
- web vs. in-store
- member vs. non-member

A key to remember is that diversification takes time, trial, and error. Don't shortchange any of them. We almost discontinued our outside snack sales because the margins were too narrow to be "worth it." In the end we're glad we've kept it because these sales are helpful for cash flow. (Coming to that conclusion took two years, expressed as Principle #9, Small and Slow Solutions.)

Variety and Possibility in Money Systems

Yes, the majority of business transactions will require dollars.

However, there are ways to incorporate a variety of money alternatives into your business. Doing so strengthens your range of possibilities and trading options, reserving dollars for non-negotiable exchanges. For example:

Local currencies
If your community offers a local currency, use it!

Hour exchanges (Time Banks)
These exchanges trade skills, hour for hour. You volunteer for an hour, earn an hour. You can "spend" that hour with another participating member. No physical goods can be exchanged (otherwise it is considered a taxable event).

You can read more about how we used an hour exchange in our community at the Georgia Municipal Association Blog. Time banks can also be a great way to build trust in your community on a person-to-person basis. (More info at http://www.timebanks.org/.)

Cryptocurrency
Bitcoin is the best known right now and, for the moment, a novelty. You might consider offering payment in cryptocurrencies as a marketing move. However, these technologies are poised to grow. Bitcoin's acceptance, use, and disruption potential shares some parallels to the Internet evolution (read it here). Keep your eyes on this.

Productivity and Power in Business Building

"Power" can be thought about in the literal sense (electricity, fuel). We can also think in terms of our personal energy reserves and ability to work effectively. Both are important.

Diversifying power in the first sense is site specific. The second sense requires tactics highly specific to your preferences and abilities. Still, we can broadly think of strategies to extend our personal power (a.k.a., effectiveness), such as:

- playing to your strengths, delegating weaknesses (to increase free time)
- learning new skills (to reduce vulnerabilities and expand personal utility)

- embracing a DIY ethos (to reduce costs)
- simplifying (to reduce stress)

Simplifying sounds a whole lot like the opposite of diversity, right? Yes, but this is a list of diverse approaches to preserving personal power. Moreover, simplification is one solution for a diverse range of problems. Clearing one area brings focus. Focus can reveal new expanse of ideas and options. Focusing also means you apply your efforts on tactics with the highest return.

What matters are the structures we put in place to support a strategy. Details are rich with diversity. (See: Principle #7: Design From Pattern to Details).

Thought Exercises for Your Business

- How can I introduce more diversity into my offerings? My suppliers? My life?
- Conversely, how can I simplify in one area to bring focus on diversification in another area?
- Do I have backup plans and/or sources for key inputs in my business?
- How can I diversify my business portfolio? (Within my business, or with additional businesses?)
- What periphery profit activities may be worth developing (or maintaining)?

DESIGN PRINCIPLE 11:
USE EDGES & VALUE THE MARGINAL
"Don't think you are on the right track just because it's a well-beaten path."

Where's the rule that says you can't have favorites?

Permaculture Principle #11 is my favorite because of its vibrancy. In nature, the point where two ecosystems meet is often more productive than either of those systems on their own. Examples would be the marshland transition between land and sea or the craggy wild between field and forest.

This quote from Rob Hopkins sums it up:

> "This principle is about recognizing that innovation doesn't come from the centre but from fringe thinkers. New business entrepreneurship comes from places with cheap rent, that tend to be cheap to rent, a bit tatty, loose and unregulated. It comes from the wild side, not from Governments or corporations. This principle is about giving status to the marginal. It is important that the business has as many fingers in as many pies as possible, as many interfaces, and recognizes that every person working for the business represents it in the community."

We Love Wild

You embrace wild and I know you love it.

The act of starting and operating an indie business is a bit of dare. I mean that in the best sense, in the creative sense. In the testing-myself sense. Hope you like emotional rollercoasters!

It is, of course, a matter of perspective. Franchisees are independent business owners, but they've chosen to lessen the risk of the wild with known policies and procedures. The price is being hemmed in and limited in choice. They are at the market whim of bad publicity from locations unrelated.

By contrast, indie businesses, especially micro-sized businesses, have exceptional freedom of exploration and expression. Of course: If it were easy, everyone would do it!

Margins of Main Street

Staying wild requires stretching boundaries. Doing so is hard, uncomfortable work that takes bravery. I propose that Main Streets are the margins in today's world. As a physical location Main Street may straddle residential and commercial sections of a city. The perception is that brick-and-mortar businesses, especially small, independent ones, cannot compete in today's world. I'm not convinced that's the case because there will always be human needs at the local level.

Permaculture emphasizes that we are in a transitional period of energy descent. The same could be said for Main Street entrepreneurship, in a different, but related, transition between an industrial economy and a knowledge economy. Main Streets are the cusp of real-life activity balanced with the market realities of (nearly) anything bought and sold online. They are at the intersection of local economies, global pressures, and disruptive technologies. Finding our footing is hard.

An example: "showrooming." That's where customer service is provided in person but the sale is made online at the lowest price. If we can't sell the widget we must sell the service and experience.

Here, the "edges" provide opportunity. Where are the edges around you? Look at the physical, the habitual, the social and socio-economic. What is here that gives you advantage over anything found with a few clicks? Serve the underserved. Create something new.

You need only to survive some wild-edge bullsh*t... You know the kind I'm talking about: those people who are clearly *not* your customer. Oh, have they got a lot of unsolicited advice to share!

This part of the edge used to drive me bonkers. Then I realized the secret. These people provide insight to my target customer. Get in the habit of asking, "Why do you think that?" when offered unsolicited advice.

Mine the diamonds, and discard the rest. (Imperfect analogy: for the record, I'd rather you *not* actually mine diamonds!)

Staying Wild

Every business has challenges, sometimes extreme, that see the shell-shocked owners running back to the familiar. Hanging out where it is comfortable is a reward for hard work. Enjoy it.

Yet, we must not become complacent. Becoming too stabilized or habitual has risks, too. We struggle to see new opportunities and sense market changes. We may become blinded to alternative solutions because "that's how we've always done it."

Staying wild means changing routine. This could be as simple as changing a daily route or as drastic as whatever is required to reboot. Here, outside interests and pursuits make a difference.

Embrace new learning and personal challenges set outside your business. Divergent interests make you more interesting, and perhaps more understanding. Both are competitive advantages to apply to your business.

Opening yourself to exploration doesn't require you to lose focus. It should introduce exposure to new and random influences. This means the conscious circulation of new ideas, new perspectives, without expectation that you would accept or use any of them.

Thought Exercises for Your Business

How are you actively increasing the input of new ideas, diverging viewpoints into your life/business? Could be as simple as regularly changing your routine in some area -- such as your transportation to your business -- to prevent the "auto-pilot" thinking and behavior. Mixing up routines can also increase possibility for valuable chance encounters and conversations.

How can operational systems overlap? For example, choosing to listen to news not to your political leaning, as a challenge to yourself, while doing a mundane but necessary business task.

DESIGN PRINCIPLE 12:
CREATIVELY USE & RESPOND TO CHANGE
"Vision is not seeing things as they are but as they will be."

The final permaculture design principle is a reverence for the fire that never ceases.

That fire is the onward march of adaptation amongst changing circumstances.

How we respond to change will determine our ability to move forward. To survive and thrive you must think of your business as an agile organism ready and willing to adapt, grow, and adjust. Working with change is easier than fighting against it. Just ask anyone selling fax machines.

Seeing changes and trends on the horizon requires active looking and observing. That brings us full circle to the first design principle. Prepare and respond as appropriate.

It would be a disservice to have a book about business building and not discuss the scariest changes of all. These are external pressures and changes you cannot control. Or the changes that require us to gather our strength and look directly at something insurmountable.

A Force From All Directions

The unpredictable and sometimes uncontrollable nature of change is that it comes pushing in from all directions. Like fire, change can be utterly destructive. Business building can be all-consuming and runs the risk of a sudden, unpredictable snap in your view of self or relationships with others. These are very real consequences. Some changes bring legitimate sorrow and mourning. Others may be impossible to navigate.

Take comfort knowing this happens to every entrepreneur.

As Kenny Rogers sang in his classic song, "The Gambler": "You gotta know when to hold 'em, know when to fold 'em."

Change could even mean closing your business. That's okay. You can start another.

Your Choice

All change -- however disruptive -- can be viewed as opportunity. It is your choice.

The "worst case" scenarios of business building (failure, public embarrassment, divorce, deep or lingering debt, bankruptcy, etc.) are terribly stressful. During our hardest days I was not taking care of myself physically, and, this had dangerous effects. I was doubling over in panic attacks, and regularly experiencing sleepless nights gripped in terror. I remember several nights checking to see if Brian was still breathing because what would happen if he wasn't?!

With time and distance this is easier to retell. It was not easy to live.

The point here is not to be a downer. The point is that our own evolution, our own personal development and growth, comes from how we deal with the toughest challenges. The best you can do is to look at what you fear directly and try to evaluate it honestly. This can be difficult to do objectively so ask for help.

We are likely view all of these changes as bad news. Trust that they are not. All of the worst aspects of business building are the foundation of learning you need to do it better next time.

Yes, there will be a next time. There is always a next time.

Changes in our lives, and in our businesses, are seasons of their own. Every winter freeze eventually thaws. You are ready for the optimism of spring sunlight. You are prepared and ready for new growth.

Thought Exercises for Your Business

- Have you rethought aspects of your business due to new information or market feedback?
- Have your motivations changed since opening your business?
- Is your business still meaningful to you? Why?
- What have you experienced that has made you stronger, wiser?
- How will you apply these lessons to your next business?

WHAT HAPPENS NEXT

Small ideas, combined and followed, can remake most anything.

My grandfather's funeral was a very sad day. Yet, no one would have guessed a stupid comment made that day would set the stage for a new business approach. Andy Sr. was a writer, so I'd like to think he'd find that scene amusing.

It wasn't the comment itself, of course. It was the agitation -- an emphasis on *why* -- that focused my mind on systems. When, in a different context shortly thereafter my friend brought up the topic of natural systems, my mind was ready.

So what happened next?

We started, one by one, thinking through each of these principles as they related to our business. We started at "Observation and Interaction" and made changes, slow and steady, repeatedly. We didn't worry about being perfect. We focused on maximizing every part of our business we could control. We looked at our strategy, systems, and tactics, asking, how can we improve the relationships and outcomes between all parts? It is an ever-evolving work in progress.

This kind of system-wide thinking turned our business around and it can be useful for you, too.

You've noticed these design principles are interrelated. You can apply them individually or attempt to work all of them at once. I think one-by-one approach forces greater thought and slower, but more likely, success. Do not be afraid to spend time thinking through your design. Implement changes over time, as it is possible.

Permaculture design principles serve as a helpful framework for thinking about your indie business' survival, growth, and contribution. Make yours the best business it can be for people and planet. *Design matters.*

WHERE THIS BOOK WAS WRITTEN
(Because Place Matters)

Staunton, Virginia
Circa 1880s rail dock "Wharf District"
In an upstairs office
After hours

THANK YOU

Thank you for purchasing and reading this book. The intersection of permaculture and independent business is unique, and you took a chance with this book. So, big thanks for downloading it and reading it all the way to the end.

Now I'd like to ask you for a *small* favor. Could you please take a minute or two and leave a brief review for this book on Amazon?

Your feedback will help me write the next book and help others find this one. Love it or hate it, I want to know! ;-)

If you'd like to be notified about the next book please join my mailing list at http://www.katiemccaskey.com.

Yours in happiness and success,
Katie

MORE BY KATIE McCASKEY

"Micropolitan Manifesto"
Photos by Pat Jarrett

Read it for free here.

ACKNOWLEDGMENTS

Many thanks to my partner
in business and in life:
Brian Wiedemann

www.ingramcontent.com/pod-product-compliance
Lightning Source LLC
Chambersburg PA
CBHW070932180526
45168CB00003B/1039